P9-APQ-811

To: AL

From: MICHAEL

Angels in Our Midst

PEOPLE HELPING PEOPLE

By Sarah M. Hupp

INSPIRE

Inspire Books is an imprint
of Peter Pauper Press, Inc.

The spire is a registered trademark of Peter Pauper Press, Inc.

*With many thanks to all of
the angels in my life*

All Scripture quotations not otherwise identified are taken from
the *Holy Bible, New International Version*. Copyright © 1973, 1978
1984 by International Bible Society. Used by permission of
Zondervan Publishing House. All rights reserved.

Illustrations copyright © 2002 Steve Haskamp

Designed by Helana Shull

7

Visit us at www.peterpauper.com

Angels in Our Midst

PEOPLE HELPING PEOPLE

Introduction

The Bible tells us that God sends His angels into the world to aid us, protect us, strengthen us, guide us, and bring us His messages of love, hope, and comfort.

In the same way, God has appointed parents to aid their children, neighbors to aid their neighbors. When we fulfill these godly appointments, we are caring for each other just as God's angels care for us.

We need angels now more than ever. In *Angels in Our Midst* you'll find real-life stories of folks just like you fulfilling God's plan for helping others. May God stir your heart through their example to show you unexpected ways to share a helping hand, a kind word, or a thoughtful deed.

~ S. M. H.

A Gift of Love

And a little child will lead them.
Isaiah 11:6

An angelic child often can lift us to our feet when we've fallen into despair. Consider the story of Casey's father. He had lost his job. In typical five-year-old fashion, Casey wanted him to feel better, so she made a present for him. She found some gold foil paper in the closet. It would make her gift look beautiful.

A roll of Scotch tape later, Casey had finished her present. But before she could pick up her things, her father walked past her bedroom. Glimpsing the scraps of golden paper and the empty tape dispenser, he scolded Casey for using so many materials, reminding her of his inability to replace these wasted items.

 When Casey came downstairs the next morning, she tentatively held the gold-foil package out to her father. "This is for you, Daddy," she said.

Casey's father was taken aback. He remembered his harsh words from the night before. As he opened the box, he began to apologize, but the words froze in his throat when he glimpsed the box's contents. He felt confused. "Why would you give me an empty box?" he asked.

Casey's lower lip trembled. "But Daddy, the box isn't empty; I filled it with kisses before I wrapped it."

The man's heart melted at her words. Casey's gift set his priorities right. He might not have a job or extra money; but God had given him something far more precious—the love of a child.

A Furry Messenger

*Be not forgetful to entertain strangers:
for thereby some have
entertained angels unawares.*

Hebrews 13:2, KJV

Ruth hurried toward her front
door. She was cold. The wind
was blowing, heralding freezing
temperatures and snow. As Ruth
struggled with her keys, she saw a
bedraggled cat huddled underneath

the shrubs by her apartment building. It gave a plaintive mew.

Ruth felt sorry for the creature, so she went inside to get it a small bowl of milk. Returning with the treat, Ruth opened the door. The cat slipped between her feet, dashed into the building, and raced through Ruth's apartment door, promptly hiding underneath her sofa.

Ruth was too tired to drag the cat back outside. "All right," she declared. "It's supposed to snow, so you can stay for the night. But tomorrow you go to the pound." With that, Ruth went to bed.

In the middle of the night, Ruth felt something strange. Groggily she opened her eyes to find the stray cat sitting on her chest, licking her face. As Ruth reached out to push the cat away, she noticed that her bedroom was filled with smoke. Though her smoke alarm was blaring, Ruth had slept through the noise.

Clutching the cat under her arm, Ruth called the fire department and then rushed to awaken the neighbors.

After the blaze was extinguished, the fire chief noted that Ruth's quick response had kept damage to a minimum and saved her neighbors from injury. "You're an angel, my friend," the chief said to Ruth. Ruth smiled knowingly. If not for a kindness to a stray cat, she might have perished in that fire.

The cat now has a permanent home in Ruth's apartment. He's well-fed, and well-christened, too, for he now answers to the name "Angel."

Doubly Blessed

He who refreshes others
will himself be refreshed.
Proverbs 11:25

Share your blessings with those
who are less fortunate. Give of
yourself and you will be doubly
blessed. These were the values that
Helen had been taught as a child. Her
family had never turned away anyone
in need. Recently a television news

story about dialysis patients languishing on transplant waiting lists started Helen thinking. . . . *I have two kidneys*, she thought. *Maybe one of them could give somebody a second chance.*

Incredibly, Helen's tissue profile matched that of a woman in the next state, a woman named Rosa. For years Rosa had worked as a nurse. Though still a young woman, her failing kidneys now left her feeling weak and hopeless. Her two sisters who had emigrated with her from Mexico were not a close enough match for a kidney transplant. Rosa resigned herself to an invalid's existence—until Helen entered her life.

The surgeries were trouble-free. Each woman recovered with no complications. Rosa was amazed. To give a kidney, a part of yourself, to a complete stranger—why would anyone do that? The only person who wasn't amazed was Helen. "Why wouldn't I?" she asked. "You don't get many chances to make a life-changing difference for someone else."

The two women had a tearful first meeting last summer. Rosa was able to resume her nursing career. Now, they are planning a trip to Mexico together. Both consider themselves doubly blessed and thankful: Rosa, that an angel was sent to her when she desperately needed one, and Helen, that she was given the opportunity to be that angel.

One Angel or Three?

Be strong and take heart,
all you who hope in the LORD.
Psalm 31:24

Children infected by HIV rarely
find adoptive homes. Dr.
Maxwell drove for two hours each
week to visit and treat infected
children, and felt exhausted and
saddened by the thought of so many
children who needed love. One child

especially—a six-month-old baby named Tommy with an infectious giggle—returned to his thoughts again and again.

In a nearby city, a young couple grappled with their own sadness. A blood transfusion tainted with HIV had shattered Anneliese and John's dreams of starting a family. They wrapped themselves in a cocoon of pain. Anneliese's doctor was more worried about his patient's depression than about her physical health.

Dr. Maxwell drove away from the children's clinic feeling more

 discouraged than ever. He began to think about his first appointment of the afternoon— Anneliese.

Could it be done? Could Anneliese and John let go of their pain and reach out to Tommy, who had never been held by loving arms? Could these three fragile human beings form a family for whatever time God would allow them? Dr. Maxwell knew he had to find out.

Anneliese and John agreed to try.

Tommy was placed with the couple
for a trial period. A month passed,
then another. Almost imperceptibly
at first, Anneliese's spirit was restored.
Tommy thrived under the care of his
new family. Love often works its
miracle in our darkest hours.

Who is the angel in this story?
The doctor who shaped this family
from his care and con-
cern for his patients?
Anneliese and John,
who were able to
transcend their grief

to extend their love to a baby in desperate need? Or is it Tommy, who knows nothing about HIV, but has found a way to bring joy into the world?

*Praise the L*ORD.
*Praise the L*ORD *from the heavens,*
praise him in the heights above.
Praise him, all his angels,
praise him, all his heavenly hosts.
Psalm 148:1-2

A Kitchen Perspective

*Each one should use whatever gift
he has received to serve others.*
1 Peter 4:10

She was alone—not by choice, of course. Her husband had died a few years earlier. Her children, now fully grown, were busy with their jobs and friends. Yet they always managed to come home for meals, for she was a wonderful cook. Often these grown children brought friends to sit around the dining table, too. Then her house was filled with the sounds of laughter mingled with aromas that would tempt any gourmet.

All too soon the meal would end. The widow would wave a goodbye to her guests and turn to wash dishes, scrub pans, and polish silver. As the

 evening shadows crept over her small home, she would retire to a worn rocker and pick up a piece of needlework, filling the hours of quiet with small stitches and prayers until bedtime.

At first this schedule had bothered her. She felt used and taken for granted. It seemed as if her children only needed her to fill their empty stomachs. They could get nourishing meals at any restaurant, she reasoned.

One evening the widow had an amazing dream. As she sat in her rocking chair, she noticed movement in her kitchen. An angel was peeling potatoes by the trash bin. Another angel stood by the counter, carving a roast. A third angel stood by the sink, washing the dishes. Christ appeared and he smiled at her and said, "Do this for me."

The widow woke from her dream with a start. God wanted her kitchen to be a place of ministry. She could be His servant, like the angels in her dream. With a smile in her heart she began to embroider these words that now hang over her kitchen sink: "No labor is common when done for Christ. Divine service is conducted here three times daily."

A Riddle

I will forget my complaint,
I will put off my sad face
and wear a smile.

Job 9:27, NKJV

*I*t costs nothing, but gives away much when used. It reflects and is reflected. The wealthy and powerful need it as much as the poor and weak. It enriches everyone who receives it without making poorer those who give it away. What is this miracle?

A smile!

A smile can convey good will in business or bring happiness to a troubled home. A smile between friends can signal a shared secret or help heal a discouraged heart. And after an awful day, when there doesn't seem to be anything to be happy about, the greatest gift you can receive from another is the miracle of a smile.

People of every language and

dialect understand a smile. It cannot be bought or sold, squandered or stolen. In fact, a smile has no value until it is given away. And though a smile takes just a moment, its memory can last a lifetime, for who doesn't remember a friend's twinkle-eyed beaming or a family member's toothy grin?

There's nothing quite as marvelous as a smile. It takes 64 facial muscles to frown, but only 13 muscles to smile. Why work overtime? Be an angel. Give away a miracle. Smile!

God's Country

Whatever you do,
do it all for the glory of God.
1 Corinthians 10:31

K irby enjoyed driving a tractor-trailer for a large trucking company. He had been assigned a regular run through what he called "God's country"–a sparsely-populated wilderness along Interstate 80 in northern Pennsylvania. Kirby drove this east-west corridor five times a week, familiar with every twist and turn, every valley and hilltop.

One Friday, Kirby was warned there might be fog along his route. The warning was accurate. One lowland area was so foggy Kirby

slowed his truck to a crawl, depending on roadside reflectors to mark the pavement's edge. He recognized a bent mile marker, recalling that shortly the road would curve sharply to the left. At the same moment Kirby saw lights in the fog as a vehicle shot past his rig. Kirby had an uneasy feeling. If the driver of

that vehicle were unfamiliar with
this section of road, he would miss
the curve.

With great care, Kirby maneuvered
his lumbering load onto the shoulder
and stopped. Grabbing his flashlight,
he jumped down from the cab and
was swallowed up in a swirling cloud
of gray mist. Tentatively, he began

walking along the curved highway's edge, listening, and studying the gravel under his feet.

Then he saw it. A smudge in the gravel. And there—a glow in the fog just over the embankment. Kirby stumbled back to his rig through the dense fog and radioed for help, then returned to the embankment and slid down to the automobile below. The driver was pinned under the steering wheel, but Kirby managed to position himself very close to the injured man. "You're hurt, but you're going to be okay," he said softly. He continued speaking gently as the emergency crews arrived on the scene.

With rescue workers caring for the injured driver, Kirby crawled back up the embankment and into his truck. He had done what he could, but he still had a job to do, a load to deliver. Then this angel of mercy would be ready to head back home—through God's country.

A great company of the heavenly
host appeared with the angel,
praising God and saying,
"Glory to God in the highest,
and on earth peace to men on
whom his favor rests."
Luke 2:13–14

Change for the Better

*Are not all angels ministering
spirits sent to serve those
who will inherit salvation?*
Hebrews 1:14

An elderly gentleman from a
small church came weekly to
the prison to conduct chapel
services. As he was not a well-
educated man, his sermons were

halting, but his heart was kind. He often brought small items like soap or candy to distribute to the inmates.

One day the old man approached Dan, who had had his share of bad breaks. Drug dealing, numbers running, and petty crime had landed the young man in prison. Dan was ready to brush the visitor off with a curse.

But then Dan looked into the man's eyes. For the first time in his life, he saw someone who cared about him, and the two men began to talk.

The old man continued his weekly sermons at the prison. He talked with Dan every week, too. When Dan had served his sentence, the old man met him at the prison gate and brought him into his home. Because of the elderly man's

faith in him—because Dan had a
guardian angel—he achieved his high
school equivalency, earned his
college degree, and graduated from
seminary.

Dan now serves an inner city

congregation, ministering to those who face the same struggles and choices he once faced. Parishioners thank him for his sermons. Little children hug his leg. Pastor Dan smiles and offers hugs in return. But a fellow reeking of cheap liquor and cigarettes receives the biggest hugs—for Pastor Dan understands him best of all.

A Generous Judge

*Even to your old age and
gray hairs I am he,
I am he who will sustain you.*
Isaiah 46:4

A widow in southern Virginia was arraigned on charges of stealing a headscarf from a department store. A judge known to be creative in his sentencing questioned her about the offense. The widow admitted to stealing the scarf because she was cold. Further testimony revealed that she had been living on the streets since her husband's death fifteen years earlier. Because her husband had been deeply in debt when he died, their home had been taken to satisfy his creditors. Without a permanent address, the woman could not receive her Social Security checks or his pension payments. She had been subsisting for years on

odd jobs—and meals garnered from trash bins.

Hearing her testimony, the judge thought for a moment. He called the department store owner to the bench for a hushed conversation. Then, to the astonishment of onlookers, the judge pulled a ten-dollar bill out of his wallet and gave it to the shopkeeper. Turning his attention to the widow, he said, "I've paid your debt. I'll dismiss the charges if you promise to report to this courtroom tomorrow morning for sentencing."

When court reconvened, the judge called the widow to the bench. He then invited two gentlemen to join them. One of the men managed the downtown movie theatre. With the judge's permission, he offered the widow a position cleaning the ladies' lounge and concession areas. Tears

coursed down the widow's cheeks as
she accepted her first permanent job
in many years.

But the generous judge wasn't
finished. He introduced the second
man as the director of the county's
Habitat for Humanity program. The
judge sentenced the widow to three
days labor helping a Habitat crew

build her a home. At her new address, she would receive her Social Security and pension payments.

A caring magistrate. A creative sentence. Could it be that this judge's robes masked angel's wings?

Angels in Disguise

I prayed for this child, and the LORD has granted me what I asked of him.
1 Samuel 1:27

Every child is God's miracle—a priceless gift that comes without an owner's manual. Yet when a baby's tiny hand curls around your finger, you find your heart wrapped in love. This small wonder has eyes that can hold your attention with sober reflection or dissolve you into giggles with a glint of glee.

The churning legs that resist diaper changes and bring bath water to a froth also kick happily against swaddled blankets. A baby's cry may signal so many things, but all can be put to rest with the stroke of a cheek, a caress on a puckered brow, or a word softly spoken in reassurance.

In many ways every newborn babe brings a small bit of heaven to earth. With perfect innocence these small ones call forth the goodness and caring in everyone around them. As God's little messengers of love, hope, and comfort, babies are truly God's angels in disguise.

An Angelic Realm

*Let us not love with words or tongue
but with actions and in truth.*
1 John 3:18

Tuesday. A day of vacation. Just what Ann needed. The laundry had been piling up in her Manhattan apartment for days. The brand new washer and dryer in the hallway will get a workout today, Ann chuckled to herself.

As the washer started chugging away, Ann turned on the television. There, on the screen, was a live shot of dark smoke pouring from one of the World Trade Center buildings. Ann watched, horrified, as an airplane struck the other tower. Transfixed, she stood in front of the television, barely able to comprehend the announcer's words.

A noise from the washing machine as it shifted in its cycles brought Ann to action. Her colleagues were in those towers! Grabbing her purse and keys, Ann hurried out the door, cell phone in hand. Dialing her colleagues' cell phones, she alerted them to the danger in the towers, urged them to leave work immediately, and offered them refuge in her Manhattan apartment.

The next few days were a blur—donating blood, buying groceries, opening the apartment to coworkers, offering clean towels to wash away the grime of destruction, washing more laundry, feeding hungry mouths, reassuring faint hearts. Days later,

when the last colleague had finally
gone home, Ann's doorbell rang. A
deliveryman held out a bouquet of
flowers and this note from her
impromptu guests:

"We often operate in a vacuum,
with our schedules so full there is
little time for interaction with others.

Yet when we yield to an inner urging, see another's need, and bring relief, it is then that we operate in the realm of angels. You were a godsend, Ann. Thank you—for everything."

Snippings of Love

The Spirit of the Sovereign LORD
is on me, because the LORD has
anointed me . . . to bestow
on them a crown of beauty.
Isaiah 61: 1, 3

Mae Tollworth doesn't know the meaning of the word "retirement." Seventy-nine and stoop-shouldered, the former hair stylist still lives on her own in a small town in central Ohio. While she no longer manages her own beauty parlor, she still finds ways to make herself useful in the community.

Twice a week she volunteers at the Guilderland Retirement Home—answering the phone, reading aloud to residents, or just providing a friendly ear.

One new resident, Rachel Muir, didn't respond to Mae's overtures. She seemed dispirited. Staff members tried to get her to take an interest in her new surroundings, but day after day,

Rachel would stare out the window, not speaking, barely eating, careless about her appearance.

Then Mae had an idea. After a quick consultation with the Residence Director, she left with a staff member in the residence van. They returned an hour later with a treasure trove—the

stored equipment from Mae's beauty
parlor including stylist's chair, combs,
brushes, and dryers. An empty
room was transformed into Salon
Guilderland. Her first client? Rachel
Muir!

Mae carefully shampooed Rachel's
hair, chatting pleasantly. She trimmed
and set the whitened locks into a

gentle arrangement of soft waves. With a final flourish from her comb and a spritz of hair spray, Mae finished. Rachel's unkempt appearance had been transformed. Mae held up a large mirror for the woman.

There was a long pause; then Rachel turned to Mae, smiling shyly. "I feel like a new person. How can I ever thank you?"

"You just did," Mae answered quietly. "That smile was all the thanks I need."

A Message of Hope

*Like cold water to a weary soul is
good news from a distant land.*
Proverbs 25:25

Radio waves can reach places no
person can. No one knows this
better than Mark Maryfield. A ham
radio operator, Mark has radio friends
from all over the world. But Ari holds
a special place in his heart.

About twelve years ago, Mark

couldn't sleep. Flipping on his radio, he stumbled across a crackled transmission calling for a reply from anyone who spoke English. Intrigued, Mark responded. In broken English, a man told Mark he was transmitting from Albania on a secret radio. He was desperate for world news. The two men agreed to re-establish contact later and ended their brief transmission.

Mark realized he had stumbled onto a miracle. At the time, Albania was isolated by Communist repression

from the rest of the world. People survived with little food, supplies, or modern equipment. Over the following months, Mark and Ari spoke often, learning more about each other and their countries, returning frequently to their favorite subject—freedom.

Like the angels in the Bible, Mark encouraged Ari to trust God for the changes that would herald new freedoms for Albania. He filled the airwaves with words of comfort, assuring Ari that his people were in Mark's prayers. Mark's words brought hope to the despairing man. Daily, Ari

prayed for Albania's independence. Mark told him that if that day ever arrived, he would fly to Albania to meet his new friend.

In 1991 Albania's Communist government fell, opening the door to democracy—and to Mark Maryfield. Walking through the customs gate, Mark saw a large gathering holding signs carrying his name and some Albanian words. Ari stood in front of the group, smiling a smile that was a mile wide. The two men hugged. Mark motioned to the signs, asking what they meant. Tearfully Ari replied, "They say you are their word of hope, their voice of freedom." And all because twelve years ago a sleepless man answered a crackled cry for help, saying, "I'm here."

Praise the LORD, you his angels,
you mighty ones who do his bidding,
who obey his word.
Praise the LORD, all his heavenly hosts,
you his servants who do his will.
Psalm 103:20–21